WORLD CRAFTS

PAPERCRAFT

Meryl Doney

W
FRANKLIN WATTS
LONDON • NEW YORK • SYDNEY

About this book

The book in which you are reading these words is made entirely from paper and card. We use these materials all the time, but we often take them for granted. Yet paper and card have a very long and varied history. In this book, we trace the story of paper-making from earliest times.

We begin with the art of handmade paper, using everyday plants and simple equipment. This is followed by some examples of the many ways of decorating paper, ranging from marbling and painting to paper-cutting.

As a material, paper has many different uses. All over the world, people use paper to make many everyday items, such as books, clothes, ornaments and even furniture. In this book, the ideas for things that you can make with paper are drawn from many countries and cultures.

Most of the steps for making and decorating paper items are easy to follow, but where you see this sign ask for help from an adult.

A chain of peace birds

The last item in this book (page 28) introduces the Japanese art of origami, or folded paper models. You could get together with a group of friends at your school or club to find out more about this fascinating art. If you learn how to fold the crane, your group could make a garland of birds as a symbol of peace and happiness.

© 1997 Franklin Watts
Text © Meryl Doney 1997

Franklin Watts
96 Leonard Street
London EC2A 4RH

Franklin Watts Australia
14 Mars Road
Lane Cove
NSW 2066

ISBN: 0 7496 2601 1
10 9 8 7 6 5 4 3 2 1

Dewey Decimal Classification 746.41

Series editor: Sarah Snashall
Editor: Jane Walker
Design: Visual Image
Cover design: Kirstie Billingham
Artwork: Ruth Levy
Photography: Peter Millard

With special thanks to Myra McDonnell, advisor and paper-maker, and thanks to Adam Baldwin, Frances Pollard, Susan Head and Rosy Dyer for paper items.

A CIP catalogue record for this book is available from the British Library

Printed in Great Britain

Contents

The art of papercraft   4
Your own paper-making kit

**Papyrus and bark —
Egypt, Australia & Mexico**   6
Make a bark painting

**Handmade paper —
India, Japan, China & Bangladesh**   8
Make your own paper

**Papier mâché — France, India,
Haiti & Mexico**   10
Make a papier mâché tray

Marbling — Britain, Bangladesh & India   12
Simple hand marbling

**Papery blooms — French Polynesia,
Europe, Thailand & South America**   14
Make a brilliant bouquet

Paper fans — Japan, China & Europe   16
Make a fantastic fan

**Lights and lanterns —
Japan, Taiwan & Tibet**   18
Make a paper lantern

**Bags and cards —
India, Britain & Sri Lanka**   20
Make your own gift bag

Paper-cutting — China, Poland & Britain   22
Make a portrait silhouette

Pinwheels — Britain & India   24
Make a pinwheel toy

**Bookbinding — China, Indonesia,
India & Nepal**   26
Make a simple sewn book

Origami — Japan   28
Make an origami hat

Useful information   30

Glossary   31

Index   32

The art of papercraft

Paper was probably invented in AD105 by Tsai Lun, an official at the court of the Chinese emperor. Before that date, important information was written on strips of bamboo or on silk. The new paper was made from the fibres of tree bark, hemp or rags. It was cheap to make and light to transport; it became instantly popular.

Almost 500 years after its discovery, paper was brought to Japan, via Korea, as the Buddhist religion spread across Asia. At first, paper was seen as a holy material and was used for written prayers or to make sacred banners. However, people soon realized that they could make many household items from paper, such as fans, umbrellas, bags and lanterns. It could even be made into clothing, window coverings and screens.

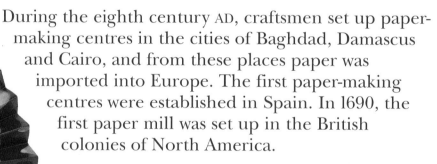

During the eighth century AD, craftsmen set up paper-making centres in the cities of Baghdad, Damascus and Cairo, and from these places paper was imported into Europe. The first paper-making centres were established in Spain. In 1690, the first paper mill was set up in the British colonies of North America.

Paper-making quickly spread across the world. Also, the methods of making paper changed as new technologies were discovered. When Johannes Gutenberg invented printing in Germany in the 1400s, a new age of book publishing began. During the Industrial Revolution in Europe, the production of paper was carried out by machines. Paper could now be produced in continuous strips that were wound onto huge rolls. This made possible the mass printing of newspapers and magazines.

The first factory for machine-made paper was opened in Shanghai, China, in 1892. The story of paper-making had come full circle to where it had begun, almost 2000 years earlier.

Your own paper-making kit

In this book you will find several simple ways to make your own paper. These are followed by ideas for decorating your handmade paper and for creating items with it.

Most of the equipment that you will need is very simple and can be found around the home. You may like to collect together a paper-making kit. Here are some of the things you will need:

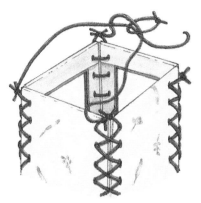

scissors • craft knife • metal ruler • brushes • paints • varnish • PVA (white glue) • tube of strong glue • sticky tape •

masking tape • card • paper • newspaper • pen • pencil • felt-tip pens • needle and thread • iron

Paper-making mould

The first thing that a paper-maker needs is a mould. It is easy to make one from an old picture frame and a piece of plain net curtain with a fine mesh.

Stretch the net evenly over the frame. Secure it around the edges with drawing pins or a staple gun. Neaten the corners, and make sure that the net is tight and smooth.

A secret watermark

A watermark is a hidden design or picture which is put into a sheet of paper while it is being made. You cannot see the watermark by just looking at the paper. Hold it up to the light and the watermark appears!

To make your own distinctive mark, bend a piece of thin wire into a shape. Sew this shape onto the surface of your paper mould with fine cotton thread. When you make your paper (see page 9), the watermark will be hidden in each sheet.

Papyrus and bark

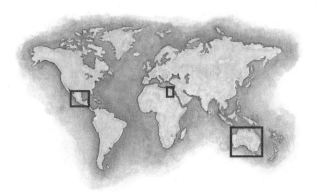

Before paper was invented, people wrote important records on pieces of pottery, wet clay, animal skin or waxed wooden tablets. In China, early books were made by sewing together strips of bamboo. The word 'paper' comes from papyrus, a reed that was first used by the ancient Egyptians to make paper. Strips of the reed are laid across each other and rolled until they fuse together to form a thin but strong paper (bottom right). The picture of Pharaoh Tutankhamun (below right) is painted on papyrus.

The Aboriginal peoples of Australia paint on tree bark. The bark is first stripped and soaked in water, before being heated over a fire to make it pliable. This decorated bark-paper bag (left) is made by the Tiwi people of the Melville and Bathurst islands off the north Australian coast. It is called a *tunga* and is worn for funeral ceremonies.

In Mexico, bark paper (below left) is made by the Otomi people of San Pablito, in the southern state of Puebla. The hard, outer layer of bark is separated from the inner fibres, which are used to make the paper. The decoration of birds and flowers is then painted by hand.

Make a bark painting

You can paint pictures directly onto pieces of soaked and flattened bark, or on paper made from bark fibres. The flat sheets of cork that are used for floors and pinboards are made from the bark of the cork-oak tree. This bark makes an ideal surface for painting.

You will need: sheet of cork or cork tile (unvarnished) • masking tape • wooden board • tracing paper • pencil • spirit-based felt-tip pen • acrylic paint in white, ochre (dirty yellow), burnt sienna (rust brown) and burnt umber (dark brown) • paintbrush • stick

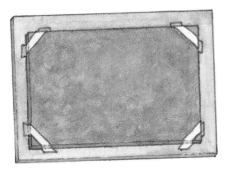

1 Tape corners of cork sheet or tile onto a board to prevent it moving or rolling up.

2 Find an idea from a book on art, or copy a picture of an animal like the opossum from Tasmania shown here. Draw your design on tracing paper. Turn paper over and pencil over lines on back.

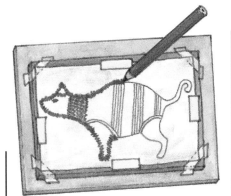

3 Tape tracing paper to cork and pencil over lines. Go over traced outline with felt-tip pen.

Add background pattern.

4 Paint flat areas with a brush. Use your fingers or the end of a stick to form the dot pattern. Leave to dry.

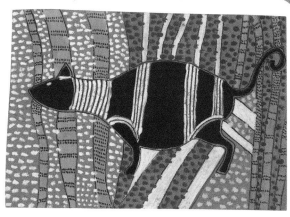

Handmade paper

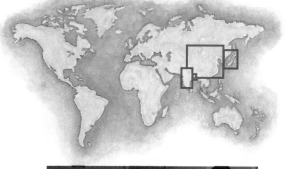

Most paper is made from plant fibres that are matted together to form a thin sheet and then dried flat. The first papers were made in China from tree bark, hemp plants or cotton rags. Most of the paper we use today comes from treated wood pulp. The plants are pounded so that their fibres break into shorter lengths. The soft flesh of the plant is then washed away and the fibres are added to water to form a 'soup'. This is strained through a mesh made of wire, fabric or bamboo strips as seen in the picture above.

The orange paper (below, far left) is made from rough coconut fibres. The papers and box of envelopes (below, left and centre) are made in India. Petals, leaves, seeds and even gold threads have been added as decoration. The papers on the right come from Japan and China. They are almost transparent. The long, shiny fibres are threads of silk.

In southern Bangladesh, a women's cooperative makes paper from waste jute and the fibres of the water hyacinth plant. This is a weed that clogs up the many waterways of Bangladesh, allowing malaria-carrying mosquitoes to multiply. By using the water hyacinth to make paper, the cooperative is helping both the local community and the paper-makers. The three tiny photo frames are made from hyacinth paper.

Make your own paper

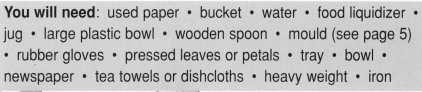

The blue paper is made from newspaper with vegetable dye used for cake decorating to colour it. White envelopes were used for the second paper. Pressed leaves were added for decoration.

You could add a watermark to your handmade paper. This method of marking paper was invented in Italy in the thirteenth century. The marks may have been a way of identifying the work of each paper-maker.

You will need: used paper • bucket • water • food liquidizer • jug • large plastic bowl • wooden spoon • mould (see page 5) • rubber gloves • pressed leaves or petals • tray • bowl • newspaper • tea towels or dishcloths • heavy weight • iron

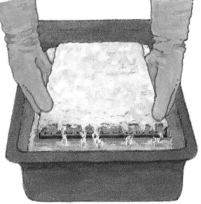

5 Place bowl upside down on tray and lay newspaper over it. Cover with cloth. Turn the mould and gently transfer pulp onto cloth.

6 Continue until you have a pile of cloths and paper. Place a heavy weight on top. Let pile dry, or iron each sheet dry between cloths. Peel away cloths to remove paper.

3 Pour one jugful of pulp and four jugfuls of water into plastic bowl and stir. Dip mould, net side up, into bowl. Pull gently upwards, catching a thick layer of pulp on the net.

4 Add petals or leaves for decoration. Leave to drain.

1 Tear used paper into small squares. Soak overnight in a bucket of water.

2 Liquidize soaked paper in small amounts until it is a pulpy soup. Add plenty of water and operate the liquidizer in short bursts.

FRANCE, INDIA, HAITI & MEXICO

Papier mâché

As the wonderful invention of paper spread around the world, people from many countries found other ways of using it. They discovered that wet paper pulp or strips could be moulded into any shape. When the finished product is painted and varnished, it becomes almost as stiff and hard-wearing as wood.

This technique became known by its French name *papier mâché*, which literally means 'mashed paper'. The green and gold tray on the right was made in France. It represents the European tradition of papier mâché when furniture and articles of great beauty and delicacy were made.

The large bowl (bottom right) is an example of traditional Indian papier mâché work. In particular, the people of India's Kashmir region have been producing fine papier mâché articles since the fifteenth century. Today, beautifully painted items like the jewellery box and the cat (below) are still produced in the region.

Other areas of the world also produce colourful papier mâché. The bus (top right), called a *tap tap*, comes from Haiti. The melon-shaped tray (top right) comes from Mexico.

Make a papier mâché tray

There are two main methods of making papier mâché. Most of the articles shown opposite were made by pasting strips or squares of paper onto a base or mould. However, you could use papier mâché pulp for the large tray. It is easy to make and can be moulded rather like clay.

You will need: newspaper • bucket • water • food liquidizer • 3 tablespoons starch glue • large wooden spoon • large plate or tray (as mould) • plastic food wrap • white emulsion • brushes • pencil • white paper • acrylic paints • varnish

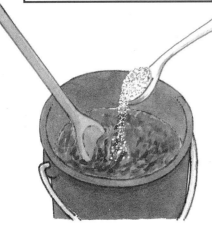

1 Prepare a thick pulp from newspaper using method shown in steps 1 and 2 on page 9. Add glue to pulp and mix to form a soft 'dough'.

2 Turn mould upside down and cover with plastic food wrap. (This stops papier mâché sticking to it.)

3 Take a handful of pulp. Squeeze out water. Pat down onto food wrap. Repeat to build up a layer 2–3 cm thick. Smooth all over the mould.

4 Leave to dry completely for several days in a warm, dry place. Gently pull dry tray from mould.

5 Paint tray all over with white emulsion. Paint second coat of coloured paint. Plan out your design before drawing it onto the tray. Paint on design and varnish.

Marbling

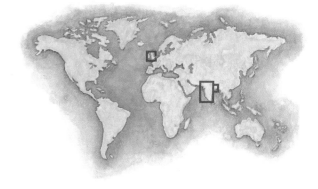

Marbling is a very simple but effective method of decorating paper. It involves the basic idea of adding oil-based paint to water. Oil floats on water, and so oil-based paint stays on the water's surface too.

This technique is called marbling because the pattern formed on the paper looks like the veins in polished marble. Marbling has traditionally been used to decorate the endpapers of hand-bound books. The example below left was made in Britain over 100 years ago. It shows the typical dark, feathered patterns that are produced when a comb is dragged across the paint on the water's surface.

In Bangladesh, the women who work at the Concern project (see page 8) not only make paper but they also decorate it using marbling. The packaging for these incense sticks (below right) has been made from a sheet of marbled paper produced by these workers.

The marbled papers (below centre) come from a factory in Pondicherry in southern India. Very rich patterns are produced using paint or coloured inks. The pencil pot is covered with marbled paper to which a little gold paint has been added.

Simple hand marbling

You will need: large plastic tray (to take a sheet of paper) • water • oil paints (at least two colours) • two mixing pots • turpentine • brushes • paper • newspaper

This method uses ordinary oil paint and turpentine. However, you can buy special marbling inks from craft shops.

1 Fill tray with water.

2 Squeeze 20 mm of oil paint into a small mixing pot. Add 10 ml of turpentine. Mix well. Repeat with different colour in second pot.

3 To test paint, load brush and flick paint onto the water's surface. If paint shrinks and sinks, add more turpentine. If it spreads too thinly, add more paint.

4 Clean tray and refill with water. Flick two different colours onto the surface. Drag paint into swirls with end of brush.

5 Place paper gently onto surface. Leave for a few seconds and peel off. Lay flat to dry. Make a second print for a paler version. (Remove paint from water with a sheet of newspaper before beginning again.)

FRENCH POLYNESIA, EUROPE, THAILAND & SOUTH AMERICA

Papery blooms

In most cultures across the world, flowers are used to greet people and to make places beautiful. Garlands of flower heads are a traditional form of welcome in many of the islands of French Polynesia in the Pacific Ocean (see left).

When real flowers are expensive or difficult to find, paper ones are a useful alternative. In Europe, rose petals were tossed on the floor for kings or victors of battles to walk on. Today, paper confetti (below) is thrown over bridal couples. Some confetti is still made in the shape of rose petals.

In Thailand, flowers are made from mulberry paper. They come in every shape and form, from lifelike roses to exotic jungle flowers (far left and below right). The paper is cut into petal shapes, which are soaked in water. Powder paint is then applied with water so that the colour spreads over the petals. Thin wires are glued down the centre of each petal.

White arum lilies grow wild in South America. The large one shown below is made from papier mâché. The small decorative lilies in the pot are made from crêpe paper.

Make a brilliant bouquet

You will need: card • pencil • scissors • white crêpe paper • white glue (PVA) • coloured inks • water • brush • thin wire • cotton thread

1 Draw a petal shape onto card and cut out. Lay on crêpe paper and draw around edge three times for each flower. Cut out petals.

2 Glue around edge of one petal. Lay second petal over this and glue again. Lay third petal on top. Leave to dry. Trim around the edges to neaten.

3 Paint coloured ink around the edge of flower. Blend colour into crêpe paper with clean water.

4 Cut 10 cm of wire. Wrap strip of crêpe paper around it and glue. Add extra paper at one end for stamen. Paint stalk green and stamen yellow.

5 Wrap petal around base of stamen. Secure with glue and cotton thread. Bend edges of petal outwards. Repeat process to make more flowers for a bouquet.

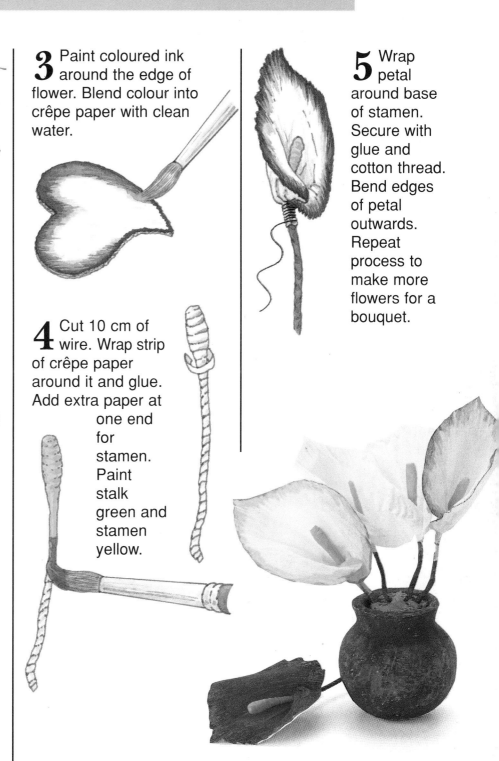

15

Paper fans

A fan is a very simple and effective idea. You can carry it around with you folded, yet it opens up into a large area of paper that moves cool air over your face very efficiently. The paper fan may have been invented in China or Japan, where it was used by both men and women. At the Japanese Imperial court, fans became a symbol of power.

A fan is also the most important item carried by an actor in Japanese traditional *Nó* drama. Fans from the Far East have traditionally been made from bamboo strips with paper stretched over them. The two larger fans on the left come from China. They are decorated with painted birds and flowers. The fan idea can also be developed into more decorative forms, like the butterfly above.

In Europe, fans became an essential part of high fashion. Ladies owned one to match each dress. They used them to hide their face or to express their feelings. In time, a complete world of social etiquette grew up around the use of fans. They were made from luxurious materials like ivory, silk and ostrich feathers as well as from paper. They were often decorated with paintings as this Victorian fan (bottom left) shows.

Make a fantastic fan

You will need: large sheet of wrapping paper • large sheet of plain paper • masking tape • pencil • ruler • large wooden board • cotton thread • sewing pin • scissors • stiff black card • small hole punch • thin wire, 15 cm long • large bead • 2 two-holed buttons • strong glue • ribbon

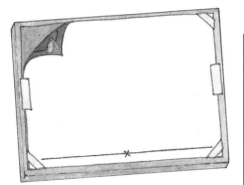

1 Tape both sheets of paper to the board. Draw line 4 cm from one long edge. Mark a point halfway along it.

2 Tie cotton to pencil to make compass. Measure 25 cm along cotton and tie a knot. Push pin through knot and into point marked on paper. Use as compass to draw semicircle.

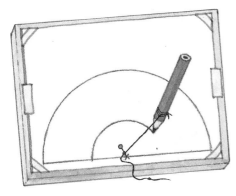

Repeat with length of cotton measuring 7 cm. Cut out arch shape of paper from both sheets.

3 Cut 12 strips of black card, 30 x 1 cm, to form ribs. Punch a hole 5 cm from base of each rib.

4 Thread bead onto wire. Bend wire in half and thread ends through button.

Push wire through ribs. Add second button. Twist wire loosely and trim ends.

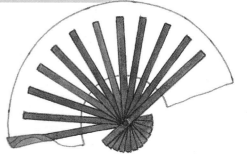

5 Place wrapping paper face down. Lay fanned-out ribs on top. Glue each end rib 2 cm from edge of paper. Fold end of paper over rib and glue. Glue ribs at equal intervals.

6 Glue plain paper over back. Fold fan along edges of ribs in a zigzag. Tie ribbon around wire.

Lights and lanterns

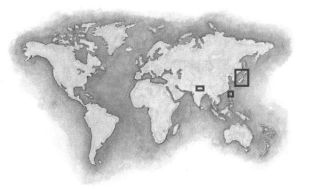

Although paper is thin, it is also strong and light in weight. For this reason it is an ideal material for making lampshades. Paper lanterns, which were probably invented in Japan, are now popular all over the world. The lampshade from Japan (above left) is made from paper that contains strands of silk.

The Lantern Festival marks the end of the Chinese New Year celebrations. The colourful lantern (above centre) was bought especially for the festival at a market stall in Taiwan. The simple white lantern from Tibet (above right) is decorated with fish — a symbol of freedom from the problems of the world.

Make a paper lantern

When this lantern is lit, it shows off the beauty of the handmade paper. You could copy the Tibetan lantern and paint the paper with a fish pattern, or use another design.

You will need: four pieces of card, 14 x 18 cm • pencil • metal ruler • craft knife • four pieces of handmade paper, 16 x 20 cm • strong glue • plastic modelling material • awl • thin ribbon • large needle • scissors

1 Draw a rectangle 1.5 cm in from edges of card. Use ruler and craft knife to cut away centre of card to make a frame.

2 Place frame in centre of handmade paper and glue. Fold paper edges over frame and glue. Repeat process with three other frames.

3 Mark dots at intervals down long sides of each frame as shown. Hold over plastic modelling material. Pierce a hole at each dot with an awl.

4 Place two frames with right sides facing out. Using thin ribbon, sew loosely up one side and down again. Knot ends. Add third and fourth frames in the same way to complete the square.

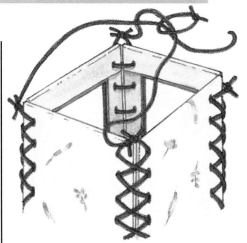

5 Tie two long ribbons to the ribbons at opposite corners. To hang lantern, attach small loop of ribbon around long ribbons.

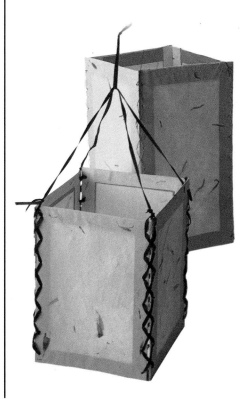

India, Britain & Sri Lanka

Bags and cards

The art of gift wrapping is not a new one. Before plastic bags were introduced, most people carried their shopping home in paper bags. In India, bags are made out of spare paper. When you go to the market to buy your eggs, they are given to you in a handmade newspaper bag like the one shown bottom right.

In many countries, the simple paper bag has developed into the more sophisticated carrier bag. Carrier bags can be made from handmade paper like this one (below), or brightly printed with a design or advertisement. These two bags (right and far right) were made in Britain to advertise a museum and a shop. Paper bags are so much better for the environment than plastic bags, especially if they are made from recycled paper.

Gift tags and cards are one way in which paper can be used to send a greeting. The card on the right comes from Sri Lanka. It is made from handmade paper and decorated with pressed wildflowers.

Make your own gift bag

The most useful paper bag to make is a gift bag. A present that is difficult to wrap can easily be popped into a gift bag. You can make any size of bag once you have mastered the technique. Try making plain bags which you can decorate yourself. Use them to advertise your school or club. You could write a special message on the bag for the person who will receive the gift.

You will need: gift wrapping paper, 70 x 50 cm • strong glue • two strips of card, 4 x 26 cm • hole punch • scissors • coloured cord

1 Fold over 4 cm of one long edge of paper.

2 Overlap shorter sides by 1 cm. Glue to form a tube of paper.

3 Fold down paper along joined edges and press tube flat.

4 Mark 8 cm from folded edge. Open out tube and fold down again, at 8-cm mark. Press tube flat again. Fold the two 8-cm sections in half, inwards.

5 Fold bottom of tube up 8 cm and open out again.

Fold short sides in and crease.

Fold top flap down, bottom flap up and glue.

6 Slip strips of card under top cuff on both sides. Pierce four holes through cuff and card. Thread cord handles through holes and knot on inside.

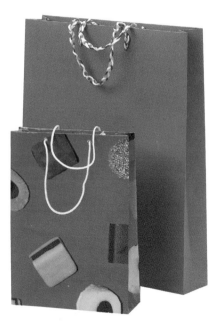

CHINA, POLAND & BRITAIN

Paper-cutting

It is not difficult to cut paper into different shapes and designs, yet in many countries of the world paper-cutting has developed into a detailed form of art. The colourful cut-outs at the foot of the page represent traditional Chinese characters. The shapes are cut from fine tissue paper which is then painted. The single-colour paper-cuts of Biblical figures and stories (below left) are made by Fan Pu of the Amity Christian Art Centre in Nanjing, China.

In Europe, traditional patterns of paper-cutting followed the designs painted on peasant furniture. The round paper-cut of two cockerels (left) comes from Poland. This paper-cut is not painted, but built up with layers of different coloured paper.

During the sixteenth century, a craze of silhouette paper-cutting took Europe by storm. A candle was placed beside the subject so that it threw a shadow onto a piece of paper on the wall. The artist then traced the profile, filling it in with ink. In France, this was seen as a poor substitute for a painted portrait. As a result, the method was named after a much hated aristocrat, Etienne de Silhouette.

By the nineteenth century, a machine had been invented which shrank the shadow so that miniature portraits could be made. This portrait (top left) was hand cut in Britain around 1950, when silhouettes were still popular.

Make a portrait silhouette

Here is a modern way of making a silhouette likeness. However, you may also like to try the original method, using a candle to cast the shadow of your sitter onto the wall. You can make yourself look like a historic person by adding a period hat or a crown!

You will need: large photograph of someone in profile • tracing paper • masking tape • pencil • white paper • black ink • pen • brush • oval-shaped card mount • photo frame

3 Tape tracing paper to white paper and transfer traced profile (see page 7). Take care to be accurate so that you do not spoil the likeness.

5 Paint the whole shape in black ink.

6 Tape your picture onto the mount and place inside frame to make it look like a professional portrait.

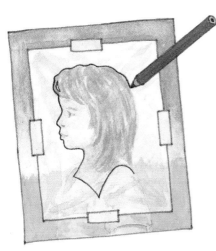

1 Tape tracing paper over photograph. Trace lightly around the profile with a pencil.

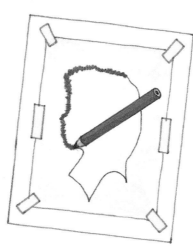

4 Carefully ink in the outline with a pen.

2 Turn tracing paper over and pencil over traced outline on back.

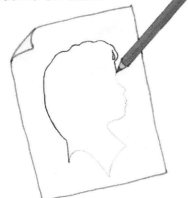

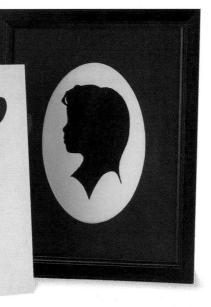

Pinwheels

When you make a sandcastle on the beach, it is only complete when crowned with a pinwheel. It is a paper whirler which makes use of the wind to whirl itself around, rather like a windmill. The pinwheels below were bought at an English seaside resort. They are made from light plastic instead of paper.

Nobody quite knows where the original pinwheels came from. They may have developed from pieces of paper hung up to scare birds away from crops, or from devices that sailors used to work out the speed of the wind. Small metal versions of pinwheels are still used to check the wind speed on the ground at airports.

In India, all kinds of children's toys are made from paper. Paper pinwheels are very popular. These women (right) are making masks and decorations. They have also made a pinwheel.

Make a pinwheel toy

Here is a method of making a single pinwheel. You could make several of them and attach them to a frame like the one shown here.

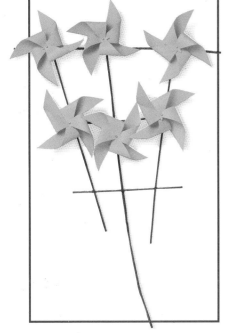

You will need: square of stiff coloured paper • pencil • ruler • scissors • long, round-headed mapping pin • two beads • sticky tape • garden cane

2 Lift one half-corner of the cut paper at a time.
Push the pin through each corner from the outside to the inside. Push the pin through the middle of the pinwheel.

4 Push pin into wooden stick near the top. Check that it whirls around freely.

1 Mark diagonal lines on the square of paper.

Cut along each line up to 2 cm from the centre point.

3 Thread two beads onto the pin at the back of the pinwheel. Wrap a 'collar' of sticky tape around the pin.

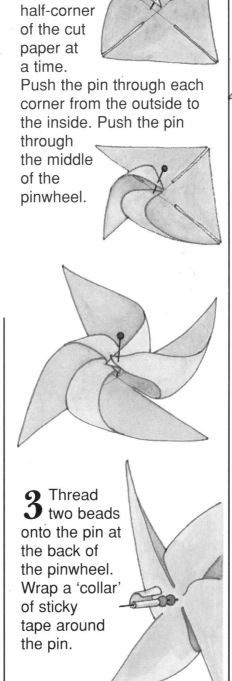

Bookbinding

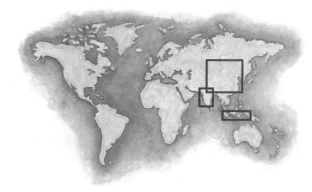

When people wanted to keep an important set of pages together to make a manuscript, they had to invent a way of preserving it. The earliest writing was done on clay or wooden boards, and later on long rolls of papyrus or leather, called scrolls.

Around the second century AD, the scroll began to be replaced by a pile of folded paper sheets that were sewn together at one edge. This technique may have been invented by early Christians, so that they could carry their precious manuscripts around safely.

Today, good-quality printed books are still sewn together at the spine, and handmade papers are bound into books in the same way. Many small paper-making cooperatives make beautiful giftbooks for sale around the world. The hand-sewn giftbook (below centre) comes from Indonesia and is threaded through with cord made from twisted paper. The book with the fish motif (below left) comes from India, and the simpler workman's notebook (right) from China.

The notebook with the bamboo strip to close it (bottom right) was made in Nepal. The paper comes from the bark of the lokta tree, which is very quick to regrow. This helps to preserve the forests of Nepal.

Make a simple sewn book

You could use sugar paper for the inside sheets of your book, as a cheaper alternative to handmade paper.

You will need: 2 pieces of card, 21 x 14.8 cm • metal ruler • 2 sheets of handmade paper, 23 x 16.8 cm • scissors • strong glue • 20 sheets of sugar paper, 19 x 12.8 cm • string • newspaper • awl • hammer • thin ribbon • large needle

1 To make front cover, use craft knife and ruler to cut a 2-mm strip and a 2-cm strip off the edge of one piece of card. Throw away the 2-mm strip.

2 Glue the card and 2-cm strip (for the hinge) to the centre of one sheet of handmade paper. Cut off overlapping corners. Fold paper in and glue.

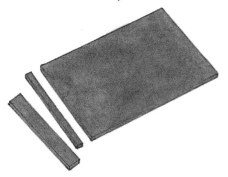

3 Glue a sheet of sugar paper inside front cover to neaten. Repeat steps 1–3 for back cover, but without hinge.

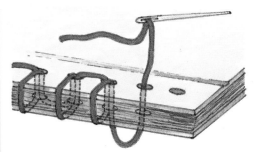

4 Stack the book with the sheets on the hinge side. Tie together with string.

5 Lay book on a pile of newspapers. Use an awl and hammer to punch a line of five holes, 2 cm apart, through card and paper.

6 Thread ribbon and sew down through first hole. Bind around spine edge and down through same hole again. Sew up through next hole and repeat process to end.

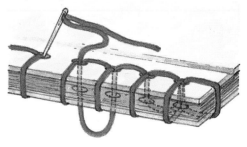

Bring last stitch up around side of book. Sew down and up along holes, filling in gaps. Tie ribbon end into bow. Remove string.

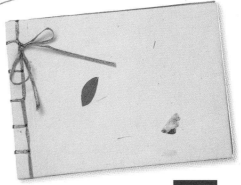

Origami

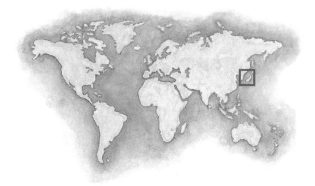

In Japan, the art of folding paper is called origami. Many of the traditional shapes are very complicated to make. It can take many years for someone to become a good origamist. Below, on the right, are some traditional origami figures: the boat, the frog, the crab and the duck.

The crane (below left) is a fairly simple design. Most Japanese children learn to make it at home or in school.

The crane is a symbol of long life and loyalty. It also represents the soul of a person. It has come to be associated with peace and with the commemoration of the terrible end to the Second World War, when atomic bombs were dropped on the Japanese cities of Hiroshima and Nagasaki. On the anniversary of this event in August each year, children make strings of small paper cranes (bottom left). They hang them in their homes in memory of those who died, and in the hope that such a tragedy will never happen again.

Make an origami hat

You will need to follow these steps carefully. Crease along each fold with your fingernail so that the folds are very exact. If you would like to make more origami figures, look for a book on the subject in your school or local library (see page 30).

You will need: a square of origami paper or gift wrap (to make your own hat to wear, you will need a square about 40 x 40 cm)

1 Fold square in half to form a rectangle. Fold rectangle in half and crease.

2 Open out rectangle and fold sides in towards the middle.

3 Open out top leaf of each side and crease to form triangles at the top.

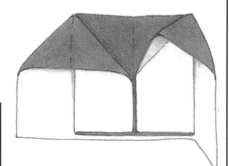

4 Fold two ends around to the back.

5 Fold the bottom half of the front upwards three times to form a cuff.

6 Turn hat over and fold the bottom half at the back up three times.

Pull hat open and make a dent in the top.

Useful information

United Kingdom

Some helpful addresses

Japan Information and
Cultural Centre
101–104 Piccadilly
LONDON W1V 9FN
(origami books and paper)

Equipment and materials

Fred Aldous
PO Box 135
37 Lever Street
MANCHESTER M60 1UX
*(mail-order craft materials,
sheet cork)*

Dryad Craft Centre
178 Kensington High Street
LONDON W8 7RG
*(paper-making equipment and
marbling inks)*

Dryad Mail Order
PO Box 247
LEICESTER LE1 9QS
(craft materials and equipment)

Falkiner Fine Paper
76 Southampton Row
LONDON WC1B 4AR
(handmade and marbled paper)

Paper Chase
Tottenham Court Road
LONDON W1
*(paper and papercraft items – other
branches across the UK)*

Wookey Hole Caves and Paper
Mill
Wookey Hole
WELLS, Somerset
(handmade papers)

Papercraft items for sale

Latin American Craft and Culture
29 Bond Street
BRIGHTON BN1 1RD
(arum lilies)

Liberty, Oriental Section
Regent Street
LONDON W1
(worldwide craft items)

Neal Street East
Neal Street
Covent Garden
LONDON WC2
*(paper lanterns and papier
mâché objects)*

Oxfam Trading
Murdock Road
BICESTER
Oxon OX6 7RF
*(paper books, fans and
Kashmir papier mâché)*

Traidcraft PLC
Kingsway
GATESHEAD
Tyne & Wear NE11 0NE
(mail-order catalogue)

Museums

Percival David Foundation of
Chinese Art
53 Gordon Square
LONDON WC1

Books

*The Art and Craft of
Paper-Making*
Sophie Dawson
(Aurum Press)

British Profile Miniaturists
Arthur Mayne
(Faber and Faber)

Making Your Own Paper
Marianne Saddington
(New Holland Publications)

*The Most Ecellent Book of How
to do Papercraft*
(Franklin Watts)

Paper (Jump! Craft series)
Hannah Tofts
(Franklin Watts)

*Papercrafts
(Creative Crafts*)
John Lancaster
(Franklin Watts)

Papier Mâché (Fresh Start)
Barrie Caldecott
(Franklin Watts)

Papier Mâché (Jump! Craft)
Juliet Bawden and
Susan Moxley
(Franklin Watts)

*The Pauper's Home
Making Book*
Jocasta Innes
(Penguin)

World Crafts
Jacqueline Herald
(Oxfam/Letts)

Australia

Some helpful addresses

Australian Paper
39 Park Avenue
Athol Park, SA
Tel. 08 347 7366

Consolidated Paper Industries
Qld Pty Ltd
98 Ingleston Road
Wakeley, Qld
Tel. 07 3390 8444

Dalton Fine Paper
11 Cressal Road
Balcatta, WA
Tel. 09 344 6611

Imperial Paper
253 Flinders Lane
Melbourne, Victoria
Tel. 03 9654 4638

The Paper House
38 Bowden Street
Alexandria
Sydney, NSW
Tel. 02 9581 1400

Glossary

Buddhist A follower of the religion started in India by Gautama Buddha.

confetti Small pieces of coloured paper that are scattered over the newly married couple at a wedding.

cooperative A group of people who work together, sharing materials and their workplace. They also share any profits from their work.

endpaper A special sheet of paper that is stuck into the beginning and end of a book.

etiquette The accepted way to behave towards other people.

fibre A thin strand or thread that is used to make up a material or fabric.

hemp A woody plant whose fibres are used to make rope.

manuscript A document that is written by hand. It also refers to an author's text for a new book, whether typed or handwritten.

marbling A design or form of decoration that is made to look like a piece of marble.

mesh The fine strands of a net or sieve. They are placed at right angles to each other, leaving open spaces in between.

mulberry paper Paper that is made from the leaves of the mulberry tree.

***Nó* drama** A form of traditional Japanese theatre.

origami The Japanese art of folding paper to make model shapes.

papier mâché A method of making objects from glue and scraps of paper or paper pulp.

papyrus Paper that is made from the stems of the papyrus plant.

pliable Bendable or easily reshaped.

profile A side view of something, especially a person's face.

pulp A soft, shapeless mass of rags, wood and other material. It is used to make paper.

scroll An ancient form of a book made from rolled paper.

silhouette A shadow or outline picture of a person or thing.

sugar paper Rough, coloured paper that is used in craft work.

watermark An invisible mark in a sheet of paper. It helps to identify the paper-maker.

Index

Australia 6

bamboo 4, 6, 16
Bangladesh 8, 12
bark painting 7
bark paper 6
book endpapers 12, 31
bookbinding 26
books 6, 12, 26–27
books about papercraft 30
Britain 12, 20, 22, 24

carrier bags 20
China 4, 6, 8, 16, 22, 26
confetti 14, 31

Egypt 6
equipment and materials, sources of 30
Europe 14, 16

fans 16–17
flowers 14–15
France 10
French Polynesia 14

garlands 14
gift bag 21
gift tags and cards 20
gift wrapping 20
giftbooks 26
Gutenberg, Johannes 4

Haiti 10
handmade paper 8–9
hemp 4, 8
hyacinth paper 8

India 8, 10, 12, 20, 24, 26
Indonesia 26

Japan 4, 8, 16, 18, 28

Korea 4

lampshades 18
Lantern Festival 18
lanterns 18–19

machine-made paper 4
manuscripts 26, 31
marbling 12–13, 31
Mexico 6, 10

mulberry paper 14, 31
museum collections 30

Nepal 26
North America 4

origami 2, 28–29
origami hat 29

paper bags 20
paper cranes 2, 28
paper-cutting 22–23
paper-making centres 4
paper-making kit 5
paper-making mould 5, 8
paper mills 4
papercraft items for sale 30
papier mâché 10–11, 14, 31
papier mâché tray 11
papyrus 6, 26, 31
pinwheels 24–25
plant fibres 4, 8
Poland 22
printing 4
pulp 8, 31

rags 4, 8

scrolls 26
sewn books 26, 27
silhouettes 22–23, 31
silk 4, 8, 18
South America 14
Spain 4
Sri Lanka 20
sugar paper 27, 31

Taiwan 18
Thailand 14
Tibet 18
tree bark 6, 7, 8, 26

watermarks 5, 9, 31

Additional photographs:

page 6 (top left): John Freeman/New Holland Publishers Ltd; page 8 (top right): Carol Wills/Oxfam; page 14 (top left): Robert Harding Picture Library; page 24 (top right): Liz Clayton/Oxfam.